The same phrase
describes my
marriage and
my breasts

Also by Amy Krouse Rosenthal

*The Book of Eleven: An Itemized
Collection of Brain Lint*

The same phrase describes my marriage and my breasts: Before the kids, they used to be such a cute couple.

[notes while they nap]

by Amy Krouse Rosenthal

Andrews McMeel Publishing

Kansas City

www.andrewsmcmeel.com

99 00 01 02 03 RDC 10 9 8 7 6 5 4 3 2 1

Library of Congress Cataloging-in-Publication Data
Rosenthal, Amy Krouse.
        The same phrase describes my marriage and my breasts : before
    the kids, they used to be such a cute couple : notes while they nap / by Amy
    Krouse Rosenthal.
            p.   cm.
        ISBN 0-7407-0050-2
        1. Motherhood Humor. 2. Parent and child humor. 3. Mother and child
    humor. 4. Parenting Humor. 5. Mothers Humor. I. Title
        PN6231.M68R645 1999
        818'.5402—dc21   98-24165
                                                                              CIP

Design by Holly Camerlinck

Portions of this work first appeared in the *New York Times, Parenting* magazine, the *Chicago Tribune*'s on-line magazine, *Digital City, Might* magazine, *Utne Reader, Chicago Reader,* and on WBEZ radio.

For Jason, for knowing that the "marriage"
part of the title isn't true, and for not minding
that the "breast" part is.

For my mom and dad, for making having a family look
like so much fun that I naturally wanted to have one too.

But most of all, this is for you, Justin, Miles, and Paris.

When my children are old enough to read this book, they should know that this is a, uh, work of fiction. Any similarities between the "characters" Justin, Miles, and Paris in this book and the "real" Justin, Miles, and Paris are purely coincidental.

Acknowledgments

(in order of height)

Paris Anne Rosenthal, Miles Barnett Rosenthal, Justin Krouse Rosenthal, Katie Froelich, Ann Wolk Krouse, Alison Scholly, Chris Badowski, Beth Kaufmann, Jeremy Solomon, Dawn Raffel, Stephanie Bennett, Deborah and Donna Broide, Chris Schillig, Kate Jacobs, Charise Mericle, Neil Genzlinger, Kay Murphy, Paul Krouse, Jason Rosenthal, Sarah Weigel, Mike Morgan, Justin Kaufmann, and Dale Conour.

Introduction

This book is a collection of observations, reflections, moments, anecdotes, conversations, quotes, lists, charts, even a couple little poem things, culled from the first five years of my 89 percent–joyous parenting journey (I calculated that the tantrums, middle-of-the-night vomiting and the episode with the boys mooning our dinner guests added up to roughly 11 percent). I suppose I could have organized the book so that all the anecdotes were in one chapter, all the lists in another, or even chronologically*. But I wanted this book to reflect the chaotic, random, all-over-the-placeness that is just part of the deal when you dwell with small humans. That's been my

---

* Because it is *not* chronological, for clarity's sake it may help to know that Justin is our oldest and is now six, Miles is four, and Paris is two.

experience, anyway. No matter how anal I get, how compulsively I sort out the toys and put them in their "proper" bin, the Candyland cards inevitably end up in the Lego bin, and *Lion King* puzzle pieces turn up in my shoes. Also, I was hoping this "short nugget" format might make it easy for a tired parent to get in bed and actually finish an entire piece or two, without falling asleep right in the middle of a sen

Blueberries

I was having as good a day as any thinking human can have. Things were being crossed off my list, work was in a nonemergency state, and there were plenty of diapers in the house—you know, the rare kind of day that even while you're *in* it, you're conscious of how smoothly things are going.

I walked in the door that night, and within seconds, my one-year-old threw up blueberries all over me.

Stickers

Every time a kid does something good, they get a sticker. They get stickers at the pediatrician. At the dentist. At school. At after-school activities. I think we grown-ups deserve our fair share of stickers too. At work, for example. "You sat so nicely through that long and pointless meeting, Ann. I'd like you to come over here and pick out a sticker." Or after sex. "Wow, honey—that was <u>amazing</u>. Here's a little Mermaid sticker." And I'll say this: If the kids get a sticker at the doctor's office merely for getting weighed and having their reflexes checked, I believe I am entitled to a sticker or two after lying there for 30 minutes with my legs in stirrups.

GOOD JOB IN BED!

YOUR OB-GYN IS PROUD OF YOU!

Handy parenting decoder

What Your Mother Says:	*What She Really Means:*
"You know, we never had that problem with you and your siblings growing up."	It was godawful for Dad and me too; we've simply repressed it, dear.
"Your kids are never like that when they're with us. Not so much as one whine."	When the children come to our house, we put on a video and feed them Gummi Bears intravenously.

What Your Mother Says:	*What She Really Means:*
"How long are you going to breast-feed?"	I can't believe you're still breast-feeding. You're a freak!
"You really shouldn't hold the baby so much; you'll spoil her."	You really shouldn't hold the baby so much; I want a turn.
"We had it easier. Our kids all slept through the night as soon as we brought them home from the hospital."	We had it easier; we didn't have baby monitors back then.

Courtesy call

Telemarketers are constantly trying to tell me that "this is a courtesy call." What an interesting choice of phrasing. Me, I wouldn't have exactly thought that the word *courtesy* would describe a call that comes in at six P.M. soliciting "Amy Krouch Rosenball" for long-distance phone service. No, a courtesy call would be more along the lines of someone with a quiet, soothing voice phoning to say, "Hi, we know it's a rough time of day in your house. Perhaps we could come by and help you chop broccoli, or throw in a load of whites, or finally put that coat of weather sealant on your new picnic table? We're also available to compliment you on dinner, give you a foot massage, sign all the field trip permission forms, and/or help raise your kids." *That* would be a courtesy call.

Even newborns get lint between their toes.

Answers to the eight questions most frequently asked by new moms

1. *Between six and twelve months.*
Anyone who loses all their weight before that is either a freak of nature, and/or Nikki Taylor.

2. *Whatever you want.*
They say chocolate, dairy, cabbage, and a bunch of other stuff gives the baby gas if you're nursing, but if you were to eat nothing but Saltine Cracker and Melba Toast Casserole, the baby still would have gas. Babies have gas. That's what they do.

3. *No.*
They don't make socks that stay on infants' feet.
You can stop looking.

4. *It's totally normal.*

5. *It's fine, just don't tell your pediatrician.*
Under no circumstances are you to unstrap your
sleeping newborn from the car seat and put her in
the crib. She will wake up immediately. Keep her
in the car seat and watch her sleep for nine hours
straight. Remember, the goal here is for you and
baby to sleep. If you're still feeling guilty, place
the car seat *in* the crib.

6. *Within one to five years.*
If you get your thank-you notes out sooner, good for you, but most people don't expect to receive one before your child has entered kindergarten. (Except for that one stray aunt who sends a message to you through your mother, "She doesn't want a thank-you note—she just wants to know if you got the gift.")

7. *Yes.*
You *will* have the desire again one day, you *will* enjoy it again one day, you *will* stop leaking at inopportune moments.

8. *Lots of love, lots of patience, and a copy of* Goodnight Moon.

Melt

No matter how Satan-like my kids have been all day, how long it took me to wrestle them into their coats, or how many Cheerios they have smooshed into the couch, I instantly melt when I see them in their one-piece fuzzy feety pajamas.

Touching photos

It all started with Michael Jordan. I met him a couple years ago (long story), and, apropos of nothing, he touched my big pregnant stomach for good luck. Knowing that the encounter could have profound significance on the life of my unborn child, and feeling that one can never really have too much good luck, I unleashed my belly on Chicago. For the last six weeks of my pregnancy I waddled around the city with a camera and asked random people I encountered to touch my bloated stomach. It was nice to have someone I had just met touch someone I hadn't yet.

Tom, at the coffeehouse

Ernie and my son Miles

A statue downtown

Sahara, a checker at Target, and my son Justin

Abraham, a taxi driver

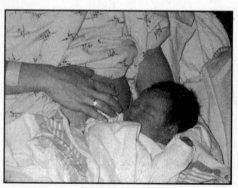

The baby, Paris Anne

Closet

We never really did the "cute crib" thing with the two boys. We just got some plain sheets and threw in a couple stuffed animals. Done. Well, we just had a girl, Paris, and we decided to go the whole nine yards . . . of fabric, that is: custom-made sheets, dust ruffle, bumper, the works. And I'll tell you, the crib looks *fabulous*.

Meanwhile, for about a month now, Paris has been sleeping in her car seat in our closet.

Can't you just see a mother octopus saying to her flock of kids, "Tell me — how many hands do I have? Does it look like I have nine hands?"

Love

I love how when we're listening to the radio in the car the DJ's banter and band names are a foreign language to them and so they get hysterical and blurt out the few words they do recognize, like "Mom, he said 'Bare Naked Ladies!'" and I love that whenever it's my or their dad's birthday, they can't grasp why there aren't any goody bags and I love that they think yellow taxicabs are really just baby school buses and I love that they refer to the exterminator as "the ant hunter" and I love that they wonder if there is specifically "a Chicago heaven?" and I love that when our flight was delayed for seven hours and *I* was a whiny brat they showed me that it was just as much fun to play at the termi-nal as anywhere else and I love that they define my job of writing as "drinking coffee" and I love that they get excited, I mean really excited, about *Jurassic Park* paper plates and I love how they can say so much with so few words, for example, "Your feelings came into my feelings, and they came and took my good ones out" and I love playing make-believe games with them where they get attacked by a tiger or vampire because then I get to revive them by slowly applying the "magic lotion" all over their soft yummy little legs and arms and cheeks and I love being wakened (if one must be wakened up) by the words "Mom, get up, get up, it's seven o'clock! WE'RE WASTING TIME WE COULD BE PLAYING!"

Regardless if they're boys or girls, all children have the "why" chromosome.

Before kids	After kids
exotic trips	...... trips to Toys "R" Us
double date	...... double strollers
hand has stamps from bars/clubs	... hand has stamp from Chuck E. Cheese

avoid looking at
pictures of other
people's kids . . . . show people pictures of your kids

you're hip . . . . you have a kid on
each hip

have sex, roll
over, and go
to sleep . . . . mumble something
about "how was
your day?," roll
over, and go to
sleep

21

walk in the door
on Saturdays with
shopping bags . . . . . walk in the door
on Saturdays with
goody bags

read the <u>New York</u>
<u>Times</u> lazily off
and on all
Sunday . . . . read one section
for six minutes
before falling
asleep Sunday night

Nose

Justin, then three, had his first trip to the dentist. Specializing in kids, "Dr. Charlie" made Justin comfortable by showing him how the chair reclined when he pressed his nose. Sure enough, when Justin pressed his little nose, the chair would "magically" move. It was all Justin could talk about the whole afternoon.

Curiously, something about the whole chair episode left me feeling sad. And then it hit me: I realized that this was the most perfect bittersweet example of how naive and wonderfully untainted my son still was. Today he believed his special nose could move a chair; in no time, he would be all too familiar with less magical things like disappointment, cynicism, malice.

We had been alternating between two CD's — "Fiddler on the Roof" and Bette Midler — when Justin concocted his first joke: "Hey, Mom — let's listen to "Bette Midler on the Roof." OK. Well, I thought it was funny.

24

Fruit

It's unbelievable how easy-going* you get with your second and third child. With the first, I sterilized anything that even came near my son's mouth. My husband would ask me what I did today, and I'd reply, "Oh, sterilized." Now if my kids ask if they can eat something that's fallen on the ground, I say, "You know the rule: As long as it didn't fall in the sewer."

Same with baby-sitters. Now, when a new sitter comes, instead of a two-page typed list of instructions, emergency numbers, and words to the baby's favorite songs, I give the sitter our beeper number, tell her which kid is which, and call out as I leave, *"Oh, and please make sure they have some fruit with their pizza!"*

*First-time mothers, please insert the adjective *neglectful* and call DCFS at once.

Can I drive a station wagon and still listen to liz Phair?

Talk

Justin's up in his room getting dressed
to play outside.
Somehow it comes up about his new friend from
school,
and how much he likes him.
I chime in about how great that is,
how lucky he is to find a good friend,
that good friends are easy to find,
but a *great* friend,
that's really something special.
He looks at me real intently.
"But let me ask you something, Mom."

He has a *question*.
I'm elated.
This qualifies as an actual dialogue,
maybe even
a heart-to-heart.
"Yes, Justy?"
> [REFLECTIVE PAUSE]

"Can I wear shorts out?"

Why do I have a turkey baster in my purse? Because
Miles was playing "Ghostbusters" and the baster, of course,
served as the "ghost sniffer" and he was carrying it
around with him all day catching ghosts, making the world
safe, but then, as suddenly as it began, the game was
over — "Here, Mom" — and so I put it in my purse.
I'm sure you understand....

Wrinkles

It started. I'm getting wrinkles around my eyes. My sister-in-law Michel said very matter-of-factly, "It's 'cause of the kids; three deliveries — of _course_ you have wrinkles." She's right: Childbirth has _everything_ to do with it. I felt better about the wrinkles for a moment. But then it occurred to me: wait — it's not like I had the babies through my face.

Waiting for the kids to fall asleep in the car so we can tear into the bag of kid-forbidden cookies

There go the eyelids.
Okay—
there you go.
Now go to sleep.
Go to sleep.
Go to sleep.
Go to sleep.

Behind every kid is a mom who hasn't had her roots touched up in seven months.

29

Eleven tiny gems

11 TINY GEMS

SPOKEN BY,
JUSTIN, AGE 3
NOTICED BY HIS MOM,
AMY
ILLUSTRATED BY
THEIR FRIEND,
CHARISE

SOME PEOPLE ARE
HOME.
SOME PEOPLE ARE
IN THE FOREST.

THERE ARE A LOT OF SPLINTERS IN THE WORLD.

LITTLE KIDS DON'T LIKE THE DARK. IT'S USUALLY HARD TO SEE.

ISN'T IT HARD TO ALWAYS BE NICE?

WE DON'T EAT HOUSES.
WE DON'T EAT LOTION.
WE DON'T BREAK THINGS.

YOU NEVER KNOW
WHEN A SNAKE IS
GOING TO POP UP.

SOMETIMES
KIDS LAUGH
REAL HARD.

I'M GOING TO MAKE SURE THE TREES ARE TALL ENOUGH IN THE MORNING.

WHERE DO AUDIENCES LIVE?

YOU CAN BE SAD
BUT NOT CRY.

I WANT TO BE
A TIGER
NEXT WEEK.

Box

No matter what toy you get a child, they always end up playing with the box. I think Hasbro or Fisher-Price should market a toy that didn't just come in a box, but *was* a box. Open up the box, and there's a box. "Wow! A box! This is so cool! Thanks, Mom! Thanks, Dad!" The kids would be happier, the parents would be richer, and best of all, the playrooms would be cleaner.

If you can cry on demand (bring yourself to actual tears, appear sad, etc.) you are either a) Demi Moore or b) a toddler.

Wait, wait, don't tell me

Miles learned the word penis no problem. (Is it not one of the first words of all little men?) But vagina, that was a tough one for him to remember. In the tub one night he asked what "mine" was called again. I said, "You know the word, think real hard." I could see him concentrating, flipping through the small but growing catalog of words he had mastered. Remembering it was both a "big" word and one that he didn't use all

that much, he proudly concluded,
"I know— spatula!"

Confessions

The kids like to suck the bubble gum–flavored toothpaste off their toothbrush bristles, and I'll sometimes count that as "brushing."

I have been known to throw away an art project or two when they're not looking.

Sometimes they'll be all excited and animated as they tell me about this incredibly funny part in the movie they watched and I start off really listening and then find myself slipping but work hard to continue to concentrate on what they're saying but then they'll just completely lose me 'cause either I can't make sense of what they're saying, or I just get terribly, terribly bored.

I forgot to bring a camera to the last holiday show at school.

Paris dropped her bagel with cream cheese on the sidewalk—cream cheese side facing down—and I picked it up, wiped off the dirt best I could, and gave it back to her.

For Justin's third birthday we got him what he asked for and nothing more: Chap Stick.

I love when we pass a cement truck because I know how happy they make you, Miles.

LOST!

my patience

Last seen with my three-year-old right before he started carrying on about not wanting to get dressed.

IF FOUND, PLEASE RETURN TO:
amy@suba.com

Test

I was just about to take the last bite of my pancakes. That completely perfect bite you savor: big piece, lots of syrup, slice of fresh banana . . . when Miles appeared before me with his mouth open wide. There was no mistaking what this meant: He felt my last bite of pancakes was rightfully his.

Being his mother—and thus *of course* possessing all the standard maternal instincts—I am biologically wired to lovingly and easily sacrifice this bite over to my son. But I was hungry and—whine, whine—*really* looking forward to that bite. Ever so reluctantly, I fed him the heavenly morsel and he sauntered off.

It was then that I realized, this, *this* is exactly the test they should give couples to screen whether they are ready to have children. *Not* how educated you are. *Not* how patient you are. *Not* how impeccable your morals are. But whether, quite simply, you can fork over that last bite of pancakes.

One of my most difficult parenting moments so far? Trying to explain to two-year-old Paris why the pigeons don't look both ways before crossing the street.

It's not just a wallet,
it's an extra twenty minutes

(keeping your baby or toddler occupied)

item	description	how many minutes it will buy you
keys	just playing with them, or trying to fit in lock	4 – 11
purse	excluding wallet	10 – 15
purse	including wallet	30 – 60 minutes dep. on child
laundry basket	dumping clothes out, putting back in – repeat	10 – 20
clasp	opening & closing clasp on highchair or stroller	10 – 20
Box of Maxi Pads	unwrapping each one, then sticking to bathroom cabinet doors	10 – 30
book	just looking at it	5
book	allowing child to eat or suck on pages	15
book	allowing child to tear out pages	60

Bathroom

It's a Saturday afternoon. The little ones are (supposedly) napping so Hubby and I go upstairs for a little Well, You Know . . .

Our bedroom door is broken and doesn't lock, so we resourcefully camp out in our bathroom, which does have a locking door.

So there we are, lying on our tile floor, and, Well, You Know—when all of a sudden we hear the familiar pitter-patter of our nonnapping three-year-old. He's now in our bedroom.

"Mom? Dad? Where are you?" He starts to cry, then sees our closed bathroom door and fiddles with it. "Are you in there?" he sobs.

We have no choice but to postpone (again) our little session, and we open the door.

"What are you doing?" he asks, seeing our pillows and blanket on the floor.

"Sometimes Mommy and Daddy like to nap in the bathroom," we quickly improvise. He accepts this without question. "Oh."

That night we're heading upstairs for bed. "Mom, can I sleep in your bathroom too, tonight?" he asks, as if it's the most natural thing in the universe.

US	OUR KIDS
Charlotte's Web..........	Charlotte's Web Site
I before E except after C	iVillage before E! except after C-SPAN
The horn on the bus goes beep, beep, beep........	Someone's pager on the bus goes beep, beep, beep
Play tag	Play phone tag

The things that somehow seem completely normal once you have kids

Paris, who at eighteen months has already developed a fondness for cool shoes, has for some reason taken to waking up in the middle of the night and asking me to put her shoes on, so I get out of bed, walk down the hall, put her shoes on, she says thank you, I lay her down in her crib, and we both go back to sleep.

Playgroups have become the Tupperware parties of the '90s.

47

McDonald's people:
You can have these ideas for free

Happy-Before-My-Brother-Was-Born Meals

Happy-to-Just-Eat-
Between Meals
(comes with pea-size
hamburger and two fries)

Unhappy-and-Whiney-
Because-I-Didn't-
Nap-Today Meals

49

You-Broke - Your - Sister's-
Hercules - Toy - Now - Are -
You - Happy? Meals

50

Happy-If-We-Can-Stay-Just-Five-More-Minutes-Oh-Please-Mom-Just-Five? Meals

Happy-to-then-hide-in-the-play-place-tunnel-until-Mom-really-loses-it-and-all-the-other-moms-look-on-with-morbid-interest-because-they-are-comforted-to-see-that-other-mothers-have-discipline-problems-too-thank-God-it's-not-just-me Meals

Sad-because-Mom-says-now-
I-have-to-stay-home-next-
time-no-McDonald's-for-me-
Something-about-natural-
consequences Meals

Happy-that-you're-loving-and-
understanding-with-me-Cause-
after-all-I'm-just-a-kid Meals
(comes with extra large
patience)

52

So does this mean he doesn't miss me?

Jason and I are away on vacation. After a couple days, we call home to talk to the kids. We miss them, and are excited to hear their sweet little voices. "Hi, Miles!" I say. "Mommy loves you—do you know that? How are you doing, my sweet boy?" There is a pause and he replies, "In *Angels in the Outfield,* a man sat on a bottle of mustard and it squirted everywhere and it was so funny, bye, Mom!"

Parenting is really not all that tough... from the perspective of experts who don't have children.

Boys

We've never purchased toy guns or weapons of any kind. We don't watch television. In fact, the most violent item in our house is the Cuisinart.

Then two toddlers became two boys. As if programmed in vitro, guns were swiftly crafted from twigs, swords from breadsticks. We always made up stories together, but now we were getting requests for dinosaurs that devour children, and nice doggies gone bad. Their most frequent question became: "Mom, can I jump off that?"

From books and other mothers of sons, I soon learned that this was considered "normal" boy behavior. I'm doing my best to accommodate and respect their testosterone, but it takes some getting used to—especially since I originally presumed we would be living like the characters in *The Children of the Forest*: you know, gathering acorns, befriending rabbits, skipping around ponds, and basically just rejoicing.

Parenting is not really all that tough... when the children are asleep.

The young and the clueless

For a long time—into my teens actually—I was convinced that when you became a grown-up, you were invited to a special meeting where all life's mysteries were explained. This was why adults knew everything and why I was perpetually perplexed.

For example, cruise ships: I couldn't understand how they could have swimming pools on them. I could only picture a big hole cut out on the ship, which meant that if you dove into the pool and the ship kept moving, you'd be left stranded in the ocean.

I asked some of my friends what confused them as a child, and I'm relieved to report that just about everyone recalled an insurmountable mental hurdle. The following compilation can best be summed up by that famous line from *Anna Karenina* (altered slightly here): Every clueless child is clueless in his own way.

"I couldn't understand the difference between a sound track in a movie, which the actors supposedly couldn't hear, and if there was a radio on in the movie, which the actors could hear. Music would be playing and I'd say to my mom, "Okay, can they hear that? Okay, now can they hear that?"

—*David T. Jones*

"If it was raining out and a fire truck went racing by, how could there be a fire? I mean, if it was raining, wouldn't the water just put it out?"

—*Jason Rosenthal*

"I remember seeing construction going on and wondering when everything would be finished—

that one day all the construction everywhere would be totally done."

—*Andy Jenkins*

"I used to think I could see atoms, but it was just dust."

—*Pat Durkin*

"I couldn't understand how people could be so stupid to die in plane crashes. If they knew the plane was going down, why wouldn't they just jump out on the wing and jump off?"

—*Greg Wojahn*

"My earliest memory of having a bath with Dad involved him covering his private parts with a washcloth. When it came time for the discussion about sexual parts with mom, I thought that a penis looked like a washcloth."

—*Vicki Smith-Williams*

"I thought the basement of department stores would fill up with steps from the escalator pushing them down all day."

—*Matt Konicek*

"Whenever I asked my parents for something, the answer was almost always 'Ispose.' I thought that was a word that meant 'Yes, you could have it, but we as parents aren't really happy about it.'"

—*Kevin Gammon*

"I thought that when my parents were little the world was in black and white because all the pictures of them were black and white."

—*Pat Durkin*

"We were driving past a hospital once, and my mom said, 'That's where you were born.' I thought she was pointing at the phone booth on the corner, so for the longest time, whenever I saw someone enter a phone booth, I thought they were going to come out with a baby."

—*Lena Garvey*

"I didn't understand that grandparents were your parents' parents. I just thought that every family got nice, old, unrelated couples assigned to them. They would then bring you presents and come to Sunday dinner. All the other kids had them too, so I figured it was some kind of rule."

—*Mike Leary*

"I told everyone in second grade that my father had two penises. I saw him run to the bathroom once without his underwear on and saw two appendages hanging there. I had no idea about scrotums."

—*Linda S. Coleman*

"I thought babies came out of boobs."

—*Scottie Larson*

The Park District is happy to offer the following classes for children and their parents/caregivers

Should you have any questions, feel free to call our offices and someone will gladly misplace your message.

Toddler Ballet

Your little angel will look soooooo sweet in that pink tutu, you could just eat her up. Basically, one big long photo opportunity. Little, if any, dancing occurs. Note: Your daughter will pull the pretty bow out of her hair right before you take the picture.

Gymnastics

All the other children will participate and look much more coordinated than your child. Actually, your child will cry most of the time and sit on the side. One hundred and fifty-eight bucks down the drain, not counting the $25 leotard.

Peewee Basketball

This is truly a great class. But you'll get to registration twenty minutes late and class will have already filled up. All of your son's friends will be in the class, and he will be extremely disappointed, not *mad,* just very, very disappointed. The guilt you feel will be monumental to the point that you will begin questioning your competency as a parent. Did we say this was a truly great class?

Peewee Tae Kwon Do

Please. Like these kids will be able to sit still for even a minute. When they start with the meditation at the beginning of class, the kids totally lose it. The teacher (*sensei*) ends up lecturing on "self-control" and "inner peace." Believe me. This is not going to work. These kids are only four years old, for God's sake. Frankly, I don't know why we even offer this class.

Peewee Weewee

This class is for those two- and three-year-olds who are new to the whole "underpants" thing. Bring them to class in a really sharp outfit and watch as they have an accident. You will then have to leave class seven minutes after arriving, because you didn't bring a change of clothes.

Little Picassos
Art projects that sound really cool, but will only hold your child's interest for about three minutes. Snack and glitter dumping for the next fifty-seven minutes.

Young Actors
The teacher, a veteran of the stage (and the little guy in that one Ty-D-Bowl commercial) takes class *way* too seriously and gets upset when the kids just want to run around and be tigers. Many of the children sprain their ankles jumping from the stage, but enjoy playing with the Ace bandages.

???
We forgot what this class is called and what exactly the kids do, but the moms all sit on the side and talk on their cell phones.

In Utero Einsteins

Give your unborn child the headstart he/she deserves. Your teacher will spend the hour playing the violin to your belly; speaking a foreign language to your fetus (choice of French, Italian, or Chinese); and lastly, teaching him/her how to play chess. If twins, please specify if you want them tutored privately or together.

Mommy and Me

For new mothers and their babies. You may say, why spend all that money to just sit in a circle and sing "Itsy Bitsy Spider" to my oblivious six-week-old? But the "camaraderie"—not to mention simply getting out of the house—makes it worth every penny. Note: If your baby is already sleeping through the night and/or you are back in your "skinny jeans," please do the other mothers a favor and stay away.

Carpooling
We've stripped away the fancy titles and fluffery and call it like it is: You carpool, the kids arrive and do nothing. This is a popular one, so sign up early!

Armpit

    I think that most of us actually go through identical stages of development: this epiphany at this stage; that revelation at that stage. So where I may have just completed the "Material things don't fulfill me" stage, our three-year-old just had the "If I put my hand under my armpit I can make cool bodily function sounds" epiphany. And I realize that someone ahead of me thinks of my new insight the same way I think of my son's: "Oh, yes, I remember when I had that one, isn't that quaint."

Rear view mirror:
The family model

SIBLINGS IN FAMILY
ARE CLOSER THAN THEY APPEAR.

Parmesan

Justin, three and a half, handed me his drawing. Very matter-of-factly, he informed me that the scribbles were (in order of appearance) a moon, a ghost, a clam, and Parmesan. I felt that this was one of the crazy but wonderful little rewards for having children; I had the distinct and rare privilege of hearing the words *moon, ghost, clam,* and *Parmesan* in the same sentence.

Driving in a minivan oozing with children, luggage, and stray toys, my husband astutely observed: "Well, we're officially a family now — we have something strapped to the roof."

If five or more of these conditions persist you are definitely a parent

1. You own a curious amount of "_____ 'N' _____" products.
(Slip 'N' Slide, Catch 'N' Count, Cap'n Crunch)

2. The same box of raisins or bag of pretzels has been in your diaper bag for at least a year.

3. You see the devil not as a red-caped, two-horned creature, but as a coffee table with sharp corners.

4. You have more in common with a stranger pushing a stroller than with some friends you've had for twenty years.

5. You've said "What do you say?" more times than you could possibly count.

6. Spit-up, vomit, and number two, regardless of color or quantity, do not faze you in the least.

7. You believe a large part of Starbucks' success has to do with those stickers.

8. Every time you open the fridge, dozens of school notices and lists fly off.

9. Lunch for you means eating leftover Kraft Macaroni and Cheese out of the pot and washing it down with fruit cocktail syrup.

10. You could seal your Double Jeopardy victory by defining natural consequences, episiotomy, and parallel play.

11. You're well-versed in the "Erbers." (Gerber and Ferber)

Amy

It's Saturday morning. One-year-old Miles is down for his nap and I'm enjoying a quiet moment with Justin, then three. Snuggling on the couch, I say to him, "Do you know that Mommy was once your age? Yep, Mommy used to be a kid just like you."

He stares at me, baffled by this notion, and after a few seconds responds with, "Is that when you were 'Amy'?"

Ode (owed) to third child

Forgive me, Paris, for all the times I went out with you diaper bag-less ("we'll only be out for a couple hours") where with your brothers I wouldn't have dreamed of leaving the house without a diaper bag stocked to clothe and feed a small country/large play group.

Forgive me, Paris, for giving away all the baby toys and the baby swing and the Exersaucer when you were, what, nine months old? Six months? I selfishly wanted my house back. Plus, you seemed so happy just playing with my keys, a box of tampons, and the clasp on the stroller.

Forgive me, Paris, for letting you still keep your pacifier. I think I'm spoiling you.

Forgive me, Paris, for saying as long as you finished your french fries, you could have dessert. I think I'm spoiling you.

Forgive me, Paris, for your baby book. No, no, you're right—baby pamphlet would be more accurate.

Forgive me, Paris, for never once actually buying you a pair of pajamas. But we have so many perfectly fine hand-me-downs. Okay. So by the time they get to you there never seems to be a matching set, but the Winnie-the-Pooh top *kind* of works with the jungle animals bottom. Forgive me also for sometimes putting you to bed in your clothes.

Forgive me, Paris, for all the times I made nice, thick PB&J sandwiches for your brothers, and simply fed you their crusts.

Forgive me, Paris, for everything I won't do with you because after your two siblings, the novelty will have kinda worn off.

Forgive me, Paris, for everything I will do with you, longer than you wish I would, because with you being the baby of the family, I won't ever have the chance to do it again.

Certificate

Congratulations!

After *five years* and *three children* you have finally realized how stupid it is to buy toys with hundreds of little pieces since they invariably get vacuumed, thrown down the heating vent, or turn up in your mixed salad.

We hereby initiate you into Phase Two of parenting.

Mother's horoscope

The month starts off unusually great: Your child will put his coat on with little trauma and the scratching and biting "situation" at preschool seems to have subsided. But by the 19th, the slightest thing sets him off: You give him the red sippy cup and he wanted yellow; he said "triangles" and you—you terrible, evil mother, you—cut rectangles; you called him "Sweetie" and he told you he hates that, IT'S NOT HIS NAME! Jupiter's proximity to the sun—coupled with his proximity to his new baby sister—is to blame. The best solution: Give it time, and give yourself a glass or two of Cabernet Sauvignon.

Special date: the 22nd. Unfortunately, however, the sitter will have to cancel.

Being a pregnant working mom means occasionally having a urine specimen hidden in your briefcase for your midday checkup.

78

Uncle Adam

Uncle Adam was over and we were all hanging out watching the basketball game. Upset by a play, oblivious to the toddler in the midst, and in full testosterone form, Adam screams to the TV, "WHAT ARE YOU THINKING? YOU GOD*#!* STUPID MOTHER-#*@ #ÿ* !!!"

Immediately recognizing a bad word, three-year-old Justin responded, "Uncle Adam, we don't say 'stupid'!"

The Pile

The Pile is taking over my life. The Pile—you know, that indestructible stack of bills, catalogs, loose photos intended to be framed, charity solicitations, school raffle tickets, and God knows what else—that has set up permanent residence in your home, most likely on a kitchen counter, dining room table, or nightstand.

Am I the only one drowning in paper? I called my sister Beth—the cleanest, most anal person I know. I figured if anyone *didn't* have a Pile, it would be her. Turns out, not only does she have a Pile, but she confided that it is the source of much marital strife. "Mark has poor Pile management," she stated. "He's got like three or four Piles going at once in various rooms." And of course the rule is: You Only Get One Pile. She longingly recalled how it was in their old place, where they had the whole Pile thing figured out. They both had their one tidy Pile in that nook by the kitchen sink. (Note: As with checking accounts, couples inevitably face the choice of either maintaining Separate Piling or going for Joint Piling.) But ever since they moved into their bigger house, Mark has been slipping, sneaking new Piles, thinking she won't find them. Cohabitating people beware: Piles can cause more than paper cuts.

I thought about our recent move. All our possessions were being loaded into the moving truck, except that collection of unpackable, last-minute items we transported in the car ourselves. This included items like flowers, children, and The Pile.

Actually *working* on your Pile can be an unbelievably gratifying experience. It offers immediate results, much like sex or emptying the trash. Granted, it will inevitably self-breed in a matter of days—or hours, but still, the sense of accomplishment is profound.

I think the average shelf life of a Pile is roughly that of a bouillon cube, which is to say, forever. I'm pretty sure it's been proven somewhere that Piles easily outlive their host.

On realizing you're trying to teach a three-year-old a term he's not quite ready for

ME *(after finding a spot in a crowded parking lot)*:
Wow! You guys have good parking karma!

MILES: Yeah, that's right—we have good sportsmanship!

With kids, everything becomes "a store." "The movie store." "The bagel store." "The soup store." My nephews even call the bathroom "The pee store."

A bumper sticker for each mood

**HAVE YOU HUGGED
YOUR KIDS TODAY?**

**HAVE YOUR KIDS MADE
YOU GO "UGH!" TODAY?**

Cameo

Please welcome my nephew, Matthew, age four . . .

MATTHEW'S DAD: Matthew, can you use your words? Let's talk about this.

MATTHEW: Okay. I don't like it when you say no.

DAD: Well, I don't like it when you make a fuss if I say no about something.

MATTHEW *(thinking about it some more)*: Well, I don't like it when you talk.

Not even a single glass remains from our bridal registry.

85

Bubble

I was chewing a piece of bubble gum—just one stick, of Care Free gum, I think it was. Son One spots the gum and bops over. "Oh, Mom! Can I have some of your gum?" I pull off a strand and hand it to him. Son Me-Too bops over. "Can I have some?" I pull off a strand for him. They're chewing contentedly, and I'm sort of sucking on this microscopic grain of gum, when they now squeal, "Hey, Mom—blow a bubble!" Blow a bubble?! I thought, isn't this, this request right here, the whole story of parenting? You give. And you give. And you give. And when you have absolutely nothing left to give, they're still standing there, waiting for you to perform that next trick.

Is it possible to go to someone else's house without getting "toy envy"? (They have great toys here. My kids don't have very ___ ___ ___ in fact "The Real Toy House.")

86

What they don't tell you: Secrets from the peewee underground

1. Your children will nap easily and like clock-work during the week, but come the weekend, you will not be able to get them to nap if your life depended on it (and often it does).

2. The night before an important event you would prefer to be conscious for, you can count on one of your children being up all night vomiting.

3. Your children will bring home lovely art projects from school that will soon amass into a great, indestructible pile because even if it is a precut paper flower that she just put one splash of fingerprint on, you couldn't possibly throw it out. This, after all, is your child's *artwork*!

4. At mealtime, your child instinctively knows that your food, while theoretically identical to his, is actually secretly different and better. So serve yourself an extralarge portion and watch her eat like a truck driver off of your plate.

5. You will hunt down the perfect Halloween costume for your child, scouring the stores and catalogs for *just the right one*; your child will be elated and wear it all week to Grandma's/to the grocery store/for his class picture; but come Halloween Day, he will refuse to wear it.

6. There is a group of informed, older children who make it a point, when your back is turned, to fill your toddler in on the evils of bread crusts.

7. Your child will often mistake you for a trash receptacle. Not only that, but when they say, "Here, Mom," and shove into your hand a gum wrapper, a hanger from the dressing room, or a chewed-up piece of food, your knee-jerk response will be, *"Oh, thank you, honey."*

8. Your hunch is right. "Twinkle, Twinkle, Little Star" and the "ABCs Song" share the exact same tune.

9. When you walk in the door, your children will jump and shout to tell you everything about their day at once. But given quiet one-on-one time together, their entire day will be reduced to "nothing" and "fine."

10. The toy that they love at a friend's house is the toy they show absolutely zero interest in when you buy it for your house.

11. They have access to a highly sophisticated, computerized tracking system that enables them to recall with confidence and precision who sat in the front seat last time and whose turn it is to sit by the window.

12. They will be able to make your heart swell with emotion and love simply by hugging a sibling, standing on a school stage, or sleeping diagonally in their bed.

Man

While on vacation, Miles, then two, and I were taking an early morning stroll along the boardwalk. He stopped to play on the stone wall dividing the beach and the walkway. Standing on his tiptoes, the top of his head barely peering over the top, he quietly gazed out at the ocean. I thought, "What a beautiful image of my child," and I walked over to be close to him.

The wall, so big to him, came up to my belly button, so I was privy to a sight he was physically unable to see. At the base of the wall was a homeless man, sleeping on the beach beneath some cardboard.

That's the essence, the beauty of childhood. Children can see only the good.

Advice

Upset with Justin (who can remember about what), I said, "Justin, sit down, I want to give you some advice." After my blabbing and blabbing and admonishing and blabbing (who can remember about what), Justin very graciously asked, "Can I now have that thing you said you wanted to give me?"

The only things my kids share easily and frequently are colds.

Eenie meenie miney moe

Whenever a dispute arises between kids (who gets the ball first, who gets the biggest piece, whose turn it is), they immediately resort to "Eenie Meenie Miney Moe." No dilemma is too big to be solved by that surreal rhyme, or its alternative cousins "My Mother and Your Mother Were Hanging Up the Clothes" and "Bubble Gum Bubble Gum in a Dish." It's really a shame that this policy is abandoned in adulthood. Then disputes turn into these long, drawn-out verbose debates where amazingly little can be decided (and I just *loathe* that pointless remark: "Let's just agree to disagree.") I say, let's bring Eenie Meene Miney Moe back. . . .

YOU: The baby's crying. Can you go give her the pacifier?

HUSBAND: I don't want to go. You go.

YOU: All right. Eenie meenie miney moe . . .

YOU: What movie do you want to see? I want to see (some movie with Sandra Bullock).

HUSBAND: I'd really like to see (some movie with guns, special effects, a prison outbreak, and/or Nicolas Cage).

YOU: Bubble gum, bubble gum in a dish . . .

HUSBAND: Let's have another kid.

YOU: I don't know. I'm sorta liking not wearing my nursing bras.

HUSBAND: Your mother and my mother were hanging up the clothes . . .

The sitter tango

When you pay a baby-sitter, there's an unspoken rule that you hand her the money while chatting, and she grace-fully grabs the wad of cash and slips it into her pocket without looking. This sequence is at the same time nonchalant yet curiously well choreographed, and seems to say, "The money is <u>totally</u> incidental here, and not at all why I spent the last five and a half hours with your sugared-up kids."

Alternatives to "Because I said so"

1. "Because I am taller!"

2. "Because, after carrying you in my belly for nine months then birthing you without an epidural because the anesthesiologist was busy with a woman having sextuplets, I *said* so, that's why!"

3. "Because while we generally agree with and try to practice the self-empowering techniques of parent-child communication, today I'm thinking my parents had it right with the whole dictatorship thing. So I can't believe it but here I am about to say the words I vowed to never, under any circumstances, utter: Because I said so!"

4. "Why do you have to? Well, that's a good question. Let me think about it. You know, you're right. You don't have to."

[When forced to really evaluate some of my requests, they sometimes seem worth revoking. I mean, does everything have to be a big deal, a lesson? Like if Miles wants to wear his favorite rainbow shirt for the third day in a row, despite the fact that it's stained more than our couch, is it really important for him to put on a clean shirt before he goes back to play at the tar pit?]

5. "Because I have toothbrushes older than you!"

Rocking

Disneyland
S t r e t c h   L i m o u s i n e s
even the Broadway musical the other night
          (and you know, that show is *all* the rave)
No.
They have nothing on

                    eating banana bread

with walnuts

                    while rocking

my daughter

              to sleep.

Breathing

When you're an adult, vomiting is this huge, dreaded, dramatic event. We say things like, "I'm so nauseous. But I can't throw up—I haven't thrown up since 1982." If and when we do, in fact, throw up, we act as if we've just lost a limb, take to bed, and send our mate out for ginger ale. When you're a child, however, vomiting is like breathing. They puke, they wipe their mouth with their sleeve, and they run back to the Tilt-A-Whirl.

We finally got the minivan. That means our "cool" second car is a station wagon.

Twenty questions

I'm playing Twenty Questions with Miles, now four, and it's his turn to guess. "Is it human?" he asks. "Yes," I say. He thinks for a split second and says, "Is it Daddy?" Not, "Is it someone famous?" "Is it a boy? Girl?" as an adult would do to narrow down the possibilities. Simply, "Is it Daddy?" This is how small and safe his world is, an entire universe comprising a few kind, important people like Daddy and — gauging from his subsequent guesses —

his brother, Justin, and Mowgli from <u>Jungle Book</u>.

Hence the expression "Immediate Family"

Sibling rivalry

There is no avoiding sibling rivalry. If you're human, and have a sibling, jealousy/tension/hatred/scratching simply becomes part of the equation. I see it in myself. I see it in my children. (Oh, not that *often*, of course; *my* children love and adore each other and share their toys without my *ever* asking.) Nothing drove the whole sibling rivalry theme home for me more than when I saw a book Justin's kindergarten class made called "What I'm sorry for." Here are, verbatim, a sampling of responses:

"I'm sorry for hitting my brother."

"I'm sorry for biting my sister."

"I'm sorry for dumping my sister in the pool."

and my personal favorite . . .

"I'm sorry for carrying my baby brother and dropping him on purpose."

Mozart

If the mailing had said, "Hey, parents—how about taking your toddlers to a place where they can't talk for one hour and they're confined to a space the size of a Cheez Nip!" I would have probably passed. But the mailing said, "The Chicago Symphony presents . . . a concert for kids!" and I thought it sounded like a fine idea. So one historic Saturday, we piled the kids in the car and took them downtown for a Beautiful Family Outing.

After exactly three minutes, Justin, then four, turns to me and says, "Mom, I'm getting to hate this."

Very disappointed by his lack of cultural sophistication and self-restraint, I dragged him out in the hall to assess the situation. Once there,

I heard a chorus of mothers yelling in that witchy-whispery-clenched-teeth voice: "We paid good money for this. We're going to go back in there. *And you're going to like it.*" Forget it. I knew *this* family had just concluded the Mozart portion of their day.

Driving home, I realized they were able to sit still after all, they really did have it in them. All I needed to do was wedge them into their car seats while wearing bulky winter coats, and put on their Disney *Fox and the Hound* tape. Silly me.

Miles gets Oklahoma and Coca-Cola mixed up. I love that.

Context

Uncle Mark came over and greeted three-year-old Justin with a colloquial "Hey, Justy, whadyasay?" Familiar with "What do you say?" in an entirely different context, Justin—albeit confused—responded with a mechanical "Thank you."

Rose garden

A friend was telling me all about this friend of hers who is the world's most nauseatingly ideal mother. She's earthy and nurturing, and she hosts killer block parties. If someone stops by for lunch she doesn't recruit random, tinfoil-wrapped leftovers from the fridge, but rather radiant vegetables and herbs from her well-maintained garden. She takes her three small children on outings to visit the elderly at nursing homes. I understand they are also looking to adopt a special-needs child. I thought a lot about her the rest of the day. I found myself energized, inspired, motivated. I found myself filled with images of all things beautiful, simple, and organic. And, alas, at six P.M., I found myself dining with the kids at McDonald's.

Interviews

ME: What does it mean to be a mom?

JUSTIN: Your job is to make sure I have food; to try to get me toys; and if I'm on the top bunk and there's no ladder, to get me down.

ME: What do you think heaven's like?

JUSTIN: The great thing about heaven is you don't have to wash your hair.

ME: You're real sweaty.

MILES: Sweating means you're having fun. It's just part of life.

ME: I'm glad you understand. Tell me one more time, what does *trust* mean?

JUSTIN: *Trust* means you don't eat the cookies.

ME: So guys. Someone tell me something cool about your day.

MILES: I farted on someone.

ME: If you could meet God, what would be the one question you'd ask?

JUSTIN: I'd ask him how the scientists invented Velcro.

Comedy club

Someone could make their fortune opening up a kiddie comedy club (though I beg you, don't spell "comedy" and "club" with a cutesy "k"). All you'd have to do is recruit a couple five-year-olds to go up to the mike and shout "Poopy!" and "Stinky Head!" and "Underwear Butt Face!" You charge a two-juice box minimum, throw some Goldfish on the table, and you're done. If anyone wants to do the legwork on this, I'll invest in a heartbeat.

What I love about being a mom,
as observed on Sunday afternoon,
5:23 P.M.

Accepting rejection

I happened to tune into the last few minutes of Miss America recently. (Or maybe it was Miss Teen. Or Miss Universe. All I know is it was a pageant, and there was an inordinate amount of giggling and hair spray.) I've always found the final drum-roll countdown to be, in the most morbid sense of the word, fascinating. It's not the winner I'm watching; no—much like the Academy Award nominees they flash on screen just as the winner's name is announced—my eyes are glued to the face of the second runner-up. How this woman is able to feign anything *remotely* resembling joy for the victor is beyond me. If anyone deserves the rhinestone tiara, it's the brave soul who has to stomach, in high heels, this particularly unique brand of nationally televised rejection.

I know I couldn't deal with it. I can't even handle it when I'm looking for a parking spot, and I mouth to the person who's sitting in their car, "You leaving?" and they vehemently shake their head "No." I internalize this as a personal rejection.

My rejection initiation started in sixth grade when Biff Pittman, my First True Love, broke up with me. The devastation was not only colossal, it was confusing; I didn't even know people broke up, hadn't yet processed that as a concept. In my preteen, prereality fog, I assumed our coupleness would go on—like summer, living under my parent's roof, and all other things good—*forever.* He left me for Kay Theory, a cute, more well-endowed catch. Eventually, I got over it, got some breasts, got a husband, but the rejection is still squirming around in there somewhere.

Being what they call "a grown-up," I must now learn to absorb the rejections my children experience, and help them learn how to process them in a healthy way. As we were driving home from Justin's new school the other day, he casually mentioned that some kid had snuffed him at recess. He was in a perfectly cheery mood, and appeared totally unfazed by his playground predicament. I, on the other hand, felt a pang of sadness. It was starting—the slow, inevitable crumbling of his safe, little world of Froot Loops and happily-ever-after. Out there, all exposed, would my dear child find happiness? Acceptance? A prom date? All I knew was that I had to prepare myself for the long road ahead: three children X the average amount of rejection = *a lot.*

Is it possible to ever get *good* at being rejected? I say no way. What I do think happens, though, is that we can come to trust that today's rejection will ultimately pave the way for tomorrow's acceptance. Rejection is like a "reality vitamin," injecting us with a necessary dose of humility (see also: David Caruso's film career). Forever the fatalist, I wonder if I hadn't been emotionally flattened by that last break up, would I have still crossed paths, at the right time, with my husband?

More tangibly, this very piece was rejected four times.

Birthdays

Birthdays, as a general concept, are difficult for kids to grasp. I remember experiencing the same confusion my kids do. For example, how can someone be older than you if they aren't taller?

older   younger   } makes sense

older   younger   } makes absolutely no sense

Also, if your birthday is "first," or before someone else's, you simply have to be older than them. Someone born in February is older than someone born in March, regardless if the February person was born seven years after the March person.

And lastly, it is mildly confusing that you can have your birthday party on one day, and your "actual" birthday on another. How does that work? Birthday = day you have your party. End of discussion.

Bad for me, good for her thesis

We were out taking a stroll the other morning and we stopped at a coffee shop. I'm at the counter ordering and I see my two little boys chatting with a woman who has all these papers spread out all over her table. I can sort of hear what they're talking about, something about taking a walk and the nice day, and she's laughing, clearly amused by their questions. Standing there watching them from across the room, I'm having what you might call a Proud Mom Moment. At this point I have to tell you that Justin, five, is at that stage where every six minutes he feels obligated to find a way to bring toilet talk into the conversation. Well, having been in line about six minutes now, I hear him say "something-something-thing-penis!" I can't make out the whole sentence, but I'm sure it ended with a loud, emphatic "penis!"

I race over, mortified and mad, and instruct him to apologize to this nice woman at once—if I'm reading her right, her facial expression says "I am no longer charmed or amused." I mumble an apology as well, and as we're walking away I catch a glimpse of the cover of what appears to be a thesis she's writing. In big, bold letters it reads:

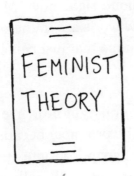

Answering machine manual: Recording your outgoing message

Now that you've hooked up your new answering machine, you'll need to leave an outgoing message. Here are some sample messages that we suggest:

Hi. You've reached the ____ family. We can't come to the phone right now. Mommy is in the bathroom and we kids are in the backyard pulling out the pretty tulips that just came up. Thanks for calling!

Hi. We're not home right now. We're at a meeting at school with the principal because one of us has been burping at inappropriate times, but please leave a message and we'll call you back. Don't forget to wait for the burp!

Hi. We can't come to the phone right now. We're in a time-out for a long time. Really long, Mom said. Like, ninety eleventeen minutes! Bye!

Hi. Thanks for calling the _____s. We're here, about three inches from the phone, but would rather not talk to you right now. Sorry, Grandma.

Hi. This is *(name of child).* This message will seem really charming to those of you with children, drastically less so to those of you without. Mommy swore that when she had children she wouldn't allow them to leave giggly outgoing messages like other parents do, but, what do you know, here she is egging me on. Not only that, but she thinks this message I've recorded is so cute that she frequently calls home just to hear my little voice on the machine. *(Child laughs.)* Have a great day!

The (parenting) game of life

You got the giggles while your daughter was telling you something "serious."
BACK ONE SPACE.

Children break coatrack after tying one of Dad's neckties to it and swinging like "George of the Jungle."
BACK TWO SPACES.

You said no Popsicles. Then you gave in and gave him one. And then you gave in and let him put the half-eaten red one back and take the orange one.
GO TO PARENTING SEMINAR.

Baby has bad ear infection; won't stop screaming.
GO TO PEDIATRICIAN.

Baby has bad reaction to antibiotic; won't stop pooping.
GO BACK TO PEDIATRICIAN. STAY THERE.

You swore you wouldn't negotiate and discuss. Rule are rules. You negotiated and discussed.
RETURN TO PARENTING SEMINAR.

You didn't know it was Pajama Day at school. Everyone else's mother did. Didn't you read the flyer?! What do you mean you "occasionally forget to check his backpack"?!
GO DIRECTLY TO MOMMY JAIL.

Daughter gets chicken pox just as you and husband land in Puerto Rico.
RETURN ALL THE WAY HOME.

You're doing the best you can.
YOU WIN.

Mother's New Year's resolution

I resolve to get rid of all your ratty, stained T-shirts;

I resolve to remember that after receiving a truck-load of new toys, what you boys ended up playing with for hours was a piece of string;

I resolve to apply, every single day, every single insightful lesson from every single parenting book and every single parenting magazine I've ever read;

I resolve to organize, chronologically, all the loose photos of you into monogrammed albums;

I resolve to keep the house tidier;

I resolve to remember that with three small children keeping the house tidy is akin to blow-drying the sand between waves;

I resolve to not stress out so much about what to put in the goody bags at your birthday parties;

I resolve to avoid the pointlessly competitive dialogue with other parents about your sleeping habits, ABC talents, and "unusually early" milestones;

I resolve to Windex our glass dining room table before sitting down to dinner each night or at least cover up the gook with a tablecloth;

I resolve to fix the porch screen door that is so badly ripped that you all come in and out of it like a puppy would, simply lifting and walking under the dangling flap;

I resolve to always keep fresh, colorful, organic fruit out in a large, wooden bowl;

I resolve to be more consistent with you, and when disciplining you, not to smirk;

I resolve to not steal so much of your Halloween candy this year;

I resolve to overpay your sitters;

I resolve to cut all of your nails and hair more regularly;

I resolve to not listen to everyone who tells me to put you down, baby daughter Paris, not to hold you so much, that I'll spoil you—in fact, I resolve to hold you more;

I resolve at least once in my life to put on a white sundress, open the windows so the air blows through my freshly washed hair and lay on immaculate white sheets next to you, baby girl, clad only in your white cloth diaper and for once, you have no oatmeal smooshed in your hair, and we look just like the perfectly calm, perfectly scrubbed mother and baby in those Downy white commercials;

I resolve to spend an entire week, from dusk until dawn, doing nothing but staring at you three children in awe of your miraculous existences;

I resolve, more often, to put your dad first.

Epilogue

ME: I don't want to talk about this anymore, guys.

JUSTIN: But, Mom—it's *my* turn to press the inside button.

MILES: No, I get to press the inside button.

JUSTIN: You pressed the inside last time.

MILES: Okay, you press the inside and I'll press the outside.

JUSTIN: I'm pressing the 3.

PARIS: Can I press this one?

ME: No, that's the alarm, Paris.

PARIS: Which one can I press?

ME: You can press the 6.

MILES: What can I press?

ME: You can press the 7.

JUSTIN: Mommy, why did you press the G? I wanted to press the G.

ME: *Justin.*

JUSTIN: Fine. I get to press it next time.

ME: Everyone happy? Can we go now?

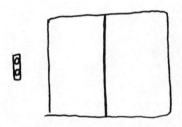

Index

(mom)e-mail

If you want to share a story or just lament about how after fifteen minutes of walking in the door, your son already lost his new baseball, e-mail me at amy@suba.com

Happy Parenting, Everyone!